FELICITY WISHES

Written by Emma Thomson and Helen Bailey

Illustrated by Emma Thomson

British Library Cataloguing in Publication Data

A catalogue record of this book is available from the British Library.

ISBN 0-340-84404-3

Felicity Wishes © 2000 Emma Thomson.

Licensed by White Lion Publishing.

Felicity Wishes: Little book of Happiness © 2001 Emma Thomson.

The right of Emma Thomson and Helen Bailey to be identified
as the authors and Emma Thomson as the illustrator of this Work
has been asserted by WLP in accordance with the Copyright, Designs
and Patents Act 1988.

First HB edition published 2001

10 9 8 7 6 5

Published by Hodder Children's Books, a division of Hodder Headline Limited,
338 Euston Road, London, NW1 3BH

Printed in China

Emma Thomson's

felicity Wishes

Little book of Happiness

Hodder
Children's
Books

A division of Hodder Headline Limited

Happiness is when
someone makes you feel
really special!

Just like a fairy princess.

Happiness is

waking up on. . .

Christmas morning!

I wonder what this could be?

Happiness is
relaxing. . .

In a bath full of
bubbles!

Don't let the water get cold!

Happiness is. . .

A full box
of chocolates!

Strawberry cream's my favourite!

Happiness is
having friends to share. . .

strawberry cake

chocolate fudge

chocolate brownies

lime jelly

oat flapjacks

Lots of yummy things!

Happiness is finishing your
homework. . .

On time!

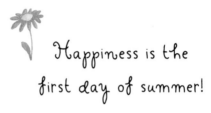

Happiness is the
first day of summer!

Is there honey for tea?

Happiness is when
you feel. . .

As beautiful as a butterfly.

And your feet don't touch the ground!

With this wish comes a special
happiness wish:

Hold the book in your hands and
close your eyes tight.
Count backwards from ten and
when you reach number one whisper
your wish . . .
. . . but make sure no one can hear.
Keep this book in a safe place and,
maybe, one day your wish will come true.

Love *felicity*